PAINTED TURTLE AS PETS

Unique Guide on Painted Turtle, Its Sizes, Lifespan, Food and Other Characteristics

Dr. Willian Monger

Table of Contents

PART 1

NUTS AND BOLTS OF PAINTED TURTLES

Painted turtles are alluring oceanic turtles with a sweeping reach in the U.S.

Well meriting their basic name, painted turtles are viewed as one of the most extreme engaging sorts of Lake Turtle local to North America. Their assortment reaches out from the Pacific coast to the Atlantic coast and from Canada to northern Mexico, making them probably the biggest specie, as pleasantly. Occupying essentially any moderate moving or still edge of freshwater inside their range makes painted turtles surely one of the greatest for the most part experienced turtles, and their distinctive shading makes them one of the most conspicuous.

There are four assortments of painted turtles: the jap painted turtle (Chrysemys picta), the midland painted turtle (C. P. Marginata), the western painted turtle (C. P. Bellii) and the southern painted turtle (C. Dorsalis). Despite the fact that their local levels differ (thus, their normal names), their propensities and hostage care necessities are fundamentally the same as.

PAINTED TURTLE AVAILABILITY

Painted turtles breed basically in bondage, and are routinely created by utilizing specialists and turtle cultivates the same. With most extreme calm species, their rearing season is obliged to spring and summer, so hostage reproduced newborn children are greatest normally accessible from May through September. Be that as it may, given the full-size quantities of infants brought forth yearly, they might be commonly accessible for limit of the year and costs are entirely moderate.

There are reports of painted turtles abiding for as much as 50 years in bondage!

PART 2

PAINTED TURTLE SIZE

Other than their alluring shading, another appealing segment of painted turtles is their sensible grown-up size. Enormous western painted turtles not regularly surpass 8 crawls long, and southern painted turtles aren't commonly huge than 6 inches. Eastern and midland painted turtles are in the middle of, maximizing at cycle 7 inches. Guys do no longer typically get beautiful as gigantic as females, anyway their size distinction isn't colossal.

PAINTED TURTLE LIFE SPAN

Painted turtles were viewed to remain insofar as 50 years in imprisonment, so they can earnestly be (about) long lasting friends. Given legitimate eating regimen, lodging, and care, you may sensibly anticipate that a painted turtle should live for 25 to 30 years.

PAINTED TURTLE HOUSING

Lodging for painted turtles can be as troublesome or as basic as you pick to make it, anyway there are some negligible lodging prerequisites that ought to be tended to. While it may be hard for most attendants to offer water this is excessively profound, the profundity need to never be not exactly around multiple times the width of the turtle's shell. A lounging region, whereupon the painted turtle can leave the water totally, complete with a magnificent relaxing mellow to help it thermoregulate, is a flat out need to.

A submerged concealing spot should be given, as appropriately, with care taken to ensure that the painted turtle can't get caught and suffocate. Non-poisonous remain or plastic blossoms might be outfitted for covering up and to rummage among, albeit painted turtles will at some point or another shred any live blossoms whether they eat up them or now not. In spite of the fact that the painted turtle tank base might be left exposed, substrate (sand, rock, and so on.) might be utilized for an increasingly home grown appearance, anyway choose a molecule length this is both too huge to even think about being gulped or so little that it will skip without issues by means of your painted turtle's stomach related tract.

Hatchling painted turtles, for example, this can be spared in a fenced in area sufficiently colossal to give 10 gallons of water, close by a takeout spot in which the turtle can totally get dry.

Since they might be dynamic and fit swimmers, painted turtles should be outfitted with a tank as extensive as could reasonably be expected. At any rate, an unmarried youngster or adolescent painted turtle should be given roughly 10 gallons of water degree. This doesn't suggest a 10-gallon tank, however as a base a 15-or 20-gallon tank mostly pressed with 10 gallons of water. Increment the amount of water by five gallons for every additional child turtle. As the turtle(s) accomplish adulthood and past they should be furnished with at the very least 20 gallons of water amount for the essential turtle, with an extra 10 gallons of water amount for every additional turtle.

Painted turtles are versatile and can be housed in really any very measured tank. Stock tanks, glass aquariums, plastic totes and yard lakes would all be able to be suitable lodging for individuals or companies of painted turtles. They can be kept up inside or out, and alright wellbeing from predators just as departure counteraction estimates must be provided in either case.

PART 3

PAINTED TURTLE LIGHTING AND TEMPERATURE

In the event that there is a decent dietary gracefully of diet D to process calcium, an UVA/UVB mellow may not be significant, yet numerous managers select to give such lighting installations at any rate. A top warmth-radiating light need to continually be outfitted over the relaxing region, and both glowing and glaring lights can give extra enlightenment if significant. For turtles looked after outside, the sun will obviously offer warmness and UV beams and no what's more lighting is essential.

Temperature slopes ought to be provided for the water, surrounding air and luxuriating district. Water must be kept up in the scope of 75 to 80 phases Fahrenheit; encompassing air among eighty and eighty five phases, and the lolling place should be kept between eighty five and 95 territories. Remember that temperatures inside an aquarium– especially if there might be a hood or cowl introduced will presumably be not quite the same as the temperatures inside the encompassing room, so it is essential to intermittently check the real temperatures inside the tank as a substitute than depending on a stylish indoor thermometer/indoor regulator. Of course, keeping up thermometers inside the painted turtle walled in area will help, as well.

Wild painted turtles love to luxuriate in the sun, thus pet painted turtles. Be certain to offer a dock or something different that will permit your pet painted turtle to leave the water completely to get dry.

PAINTED TURTLE FOOD

Painted turtles are omnivorous, and will acknowledge both creature and plant depend with indistinguishable excitement. Alongside fish, worms and creepy crawlies, give them green, verdant veggies and oceanic plants comprehensive of water lettuce, water hyacinth and duckweed. Notwithstanding live and common nourishments, there's a wide style of business turtle food accessible at the market, and greatest had been planned to give most beneficial supplements to turtles at all degrees of development. Focus on viewpoint marks; I suggest abstains from food with the accompanying: 30-to 40-percent protein; low fats content; nutrient D and a high calcium-to-phosphorous proportion. I additionally propose diet and mineral supplementation.

PART 4

PAINTED TURTLE HEALTH

Furnished with appropriate lodging and diet, painted turtles are dynamic and dynamic pets. In any case, similarly as with each creature, sickness and disease can affect them. A few indications of wellness inconveniences include: swollen or indented eyes; posting or inability to lower; expanding or foaming at the mouth, or air pockets inside the nose; unbalanced lounging or refusal to enter the water; absence of capacity or refusal to take care of; topsy-turvy or unpredictable development; evident staining or open injuries at the pores and skin or shell; or some other abnormal appearance or conduct. On the off chance that your painted turtle uncovers any of these issues, veterinary consideration is suggested. Be certain to utilize a vet that has practical experience in turtles and tortoises, or as a base reptiles and particular creatures. A rundown of reptile vets can be seen here.

Albeit now not unquestionably social creatures, painted turtles are gregarious and ready to cohabitating with turtles of their own and various species with equivalent lodging needs. Both genders are equipped for predominant or regional animosity, yet as long as satisfactory space and concealing locales are provided, this direct is generally not, at this point serious adequate to achieve outrageous injury. In any case, if consistent hostility is noted, it can be indispensable to give bigger natural surroundings or even totally segregate affronting turtles.

Painted turtles aren't trained creatures that flourish with human warmth and contact, so they have to now not be dealt with aside from as of need. Regardless of appearances in actuality, overseeing is stressing to the painted turtle and subjects the handler to gnawing and scratching by utilizing the turtle. Incidental managing to assess a painted turtle for wellbeing or wounds, and once in a while moving painted turtles to trade pressing compartments during cleaning and redesign of their essential living space, is worthy. As continually, a concentrated hand-washing with cleanser and warm water when a turtle or any related materials or gear has been managed will assist with avoiding any ailment transmission among human and turtle.

THE END

www.ingramcontent.com/pod-product-compliance
Lightning Source LLC
Chambersburg PA
CBHW072146150726
48002CB00004B/1659